Collins

easy lea[rning]

Gaelic

Ages 7-11

Halò!

Ciamar a tha thu?

Is mise
My name is

A' cleachdadh an leabhair seo
Using this book

- Look at the left-hand page first to familiarise yourself with the vocabulary being covered.
- There are links to audio files online to help you learn how to say Gaelic words, as well as pronunciations given in the text as a general guide to help you. Where the letters **ch** appear in bold type, you should pronounce this like the "**ch**" sound in Scottish "lo**ch**". Where the letter **g** appears in bold type, this should sound like a slightly rasped hard "g" sound…a bit like the beginning of a gargle, only without any water! The online audio will help you with these trickier sounds.
- Read out the instructions clearly and ensure children understand what they have to do.
- Discuss with the children what they have learnt and return to topics that they have enjoyed.
- Reward children with plenty of praise and encouragement.
- Encourage children to say new words out loud. This will help them to practise speaking Gaelic, and help them to remember new words.
- Make learning Gaelic fun for you and your children!

Special features

- Yellow boxes: introduce and outline the key vocabulary and structures in Gaelic.
- Orange boxes: offer suggestions for other activities for children to consolidate their learning in different contexts.
- Orange shaded boxes: provide additional information about Gaelic language and culture.
- Blue boxes: give instructions for an activity to reinforce learning.
- Audio symbols (🔊): indicate where further resources and support are available online at www.collins.co.uk/homeworkhelp

HarperCollins Publishers
Westerhill Road
Bishopbriggs
Glasgow
G64 2QT

First Edition 2020

10 9 8 7 6 5 4 3 2 1

© HarperCollins Publishers 2020

ISBN 978-0-00-838944-4

www.collins.co.uk

Printed and bound in
the UK by Martins the Printer Ltd

All rights reserved. No part of this book may be reproduced, stored in a retrieval system, or transmitted in any form or by any means, electronic, mechanical, photocopying, recording or otherwise, without the prior permission in writing of the Publisher. This book is sold subject to the conditions that it shall not, by way of trade or otherwise, be lent, re-sold, hired out or otherwise circulated without the Publisher's prior consent in any form of binding or cover other than that in which it is published and without a similar condition including this condition being imposed on the subsequent purchaser.

The contents of this publication are believed correct at the time of printing. Nevertheless the Publisher can accept no responsibility for errors or omissions, changes in the detail given or for any expense or loss thereby caused.

A catalogue record for this book is available from the British Library.

MANAGING EDITOR
Maree Airlie

FOR THE PUBLISHER
Michelle I'Anson
Gina Macleod
Sarah Woods

CONTRIBUTORS
Mairi Maclean

ILLUSTRATIONS
All Q2A Media, except:
p22 strawberry jam;
p22 roast chicken;
p30 MacKillop tartan;
p30 musical notes: Shutterstock.com
p18 calendar: Maria Herbert-Liew

MAPS
© Collins Bartholomew Ltd

COVER IMAGE
Shutterstock
© Portare fortuna

Chuidich Comhairle nan Leabhraichean am foillsichear le cosgaisean an leabhair agus na clàraidhean seo.

MIX
Paper from responsible sources
FSC™ C007454

This book is produced from independently certified FSC™ paper to ensure responsible forest management.

For more information visit: www.harpercollins.co.uk/green

Clàr-innse
Contents

A' cleachdadh an leabhair seo
Using this book — 2

Faclan feumail
Useful words — 4

Cò thu?
Who are you? — 6

Seo mo theaghlach
This is my family — 8

Cò ris a tha mi coltach?
What do I look like? — 10

Tha mi a' faireachdainn...
I feel... — 12

An aimsir
The weather — 14

Àireamhan gu 100
Numbers to 100 — 16

Làithean na seachdaine/Mìosan
Days of the week/Months — 18

Cur-seachadan
Pastimes — 20

Biadh
Food — 22

Deoch
Drink — 24

Na rudan as fheàrr leam
My favourite things — 26

Mi fhìn
About me — 28

Traidiseanan agus cultar
Traditions and culture — 30

Cumaibh oirbh!
Keep going! — 31

Faclan feumail
Useful words

Whether you've already started learning Gaelic, or have only just begun, this vocabulary will be useful for you to practise. Why not cover the pictures up and see if you can remember the Gaelic words? Find audio recordings to help you with this vocabulary at the Ages 5-7 section on our website: www.collins.co.uk/homeworkhelp

When you first start speaking Gaelic you want to be able to say some simple things to people you meet:

Halò! [hallo] **Hello!**

Ciamar a tha thu? [kimar uh haa oo] **How are you?**

Tha gu math, tapadh leat. [haa goo mah, tapuh lat] **Fine, thanks.**

Haidh! [hi] **Hi!**

Dè an t-ainm a th' ort? [jay un tannam uh horst] **What's your name?**

Is mise Eilidh. [iss mishuh aylee] **I'm Eilidh.**

Mar sin leat! [mar shin lat] **Goodbye!**

Tìoraidh! [cheery] **Bye!**

Here are the numbers you need to count up to 20 in Gaelic:

| 1 aon [unn] | 2 dhà [gaa] | 3 trì [tree] | 4 ceithir [kayher] | 5 còig [koeek] | 6 sia [shia] | 7 seachd [shachk] | 8 ochd [ochk] | 9 naoi [nuee] | 10 deich [jaych] |

| 11 aon-deug [unn jeeuck] | 12 dhà-dheug [gaa yeeuck] | 13 trì-deug [tree jeeuck] | 14 ceithir-deug [kayher jeeuck] | 15 còig-deug [koeek jeeuck] | 16 sia-deug [shia jeeuck] | 17 seachd-deug [shachk jeeuck] | 18 ochd-deug [ochk jeeuck] | 19 naoi-deug [nuee jeeuck] | 20 fichead [feechit] |

Use these words to introduce some members of your family:

Seo... [shaw] **This is...**

...mo **mhamaidh** [mo vamee] ...my mummy

...mo **phiuthar** [mo fyoower] ...my sister

...mo **sheanmhair** [mo henavar] ...my granny

...mo **dhadaidh** [mo gadee] ...my daddy

...mo **bhràthair** [mo vraaher] ...my brother

...mo **sheanair** [mo henar] ...my grandad

These are the names of some colours in Gaelic:

gorm [gorrum]   **dearg** [jerrack]   **uaine** [ooanyuh]   **buidhe** [booyuh]   **geal** [gyal]   **dubh** [doo]   **pinc** [pink]   **purpaidh** [poorpee]   **orains** [orensh]   **donn** [down]

Here are the Gaelic words for pets that you might have:

cù [koo] dog

òr-iasg [orr eeusk] goldfish

rabaid [rabatch] rabbit

hamstair [hamstur] hamster

cat [kat] cat

gearra-mhuc [gyarra vook] guinea pig

sligeanach [shleekana**ch**] tortoise

each [e**ch**] horse

It's useful to know the Gaelic words for parts of your body:

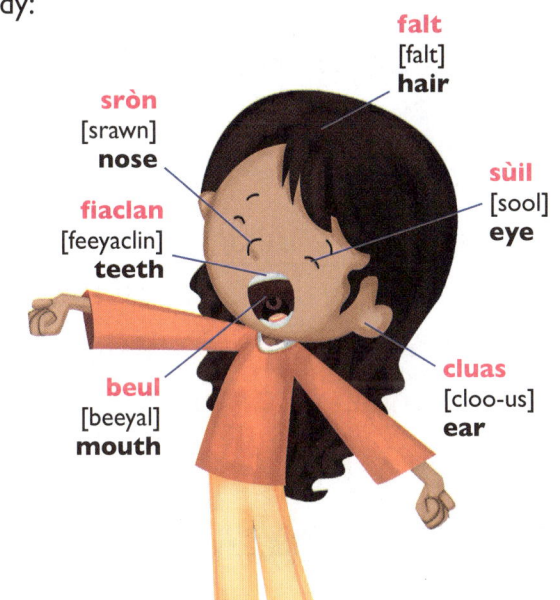

aodann [uhdan] face

gualann [goo-uh-lun] shoulder

gàirdean [gaarshdan] arm

làmh [laav] hand

cas [kass] foot

ceann [kya-oon] head

corrag [korrack] finger

stamag [stammack] tummy

glùin [glooeen] knee

cas [kass] leg

falt [falt] hair

sròn [srawn] nose

fiaclan [feeyaclin] teeth

beul [beeyal] mouth

sùil [sool] eye

cluas [cloo-us] ear

Here are some of the things you might need at school:

peann [pya-oon] pen

peansail [pensal] pencil

rubair [rubbar] rubber

poca-peansail [pokuh pensal] pencil case

geuradair [geeyaredar] sharpener

rùilear [roolar] ruler

Cò thu?
Who are you?

As well as being able to say hello to someone and tell them your name, you may want to talk about how old you are.

Halò! Is mise Anndra.
[hallo, iss mishuh aa-oondra]
Hello! I'm Anndra.

Haidh! Is mise Emma.
[hi, iss mishuh emma]
Hi! I'm Emma.

Tha mi ochd bliadhna a dh'aois.
[haa mee och**k** bleeyunuh uh **g**oosh]
I'm eight years old.

Dè an aois a tha thu?
[jay un oosh uh haa oo]
How old are you?

Dè an aois a tha thu fhèin?
[jay un oosh uh haa oo hayn]
And how old are you?

Tha mi deich bliadhna a dh'aois.
[haa mee jay**ch** bleeyunuh uh **g**oosh]
I'm ten years old.

🔊 Listen to Track 1 / **Èist ri Traca 1**

When you are talking about your age, use the phrase **Tha mi ... bliadhna a dh'aois** [haa mee ... bleeyunuh uh **g**oosh] which means **I am ... years old**. **Tha mi naoi bliadhna a dh'aois** [haa mee nuee bleeyunuh uh **g**oosh] means **I am nine years old**. To ask someone their age, you say **Dè an aois a tha thu?** [jay un oosh uh haa oo].

Make finger puppets or draw faces on your fingers and give each one a name and age. Have a conversation between your fingers or with a partner's fingers.

Do you know...? A bheil fios agad...? The question **Dè an t-ainm a th' ort?** [jay un tannam uh horst] is how you ask someone their name in Gaelic; in English, the word-by-word translation is **What is the name on you?**

You are talking to a new friend. Only their half of the conversation is written down. Fill in your missing greeting words and answers.

Halò! _____!

Dè an t-ainm a th' ort? _____

Dè an aois a tha thu? _____

Mar sin leat! _____!

Draw a cartoon strip of two characters meeting and finding out about each other. You can use animals or cartoon characters if you prefer. Use the language you have been learning to write speech bubbles.

1.

2.

3.

4.

Seo mo theaghlach
This is my family

The word for **father** or **dad** in Gaelic is **athair** [aher] and the word **bràthair** [braaher] means **brother**. Here is how you say **my father/brother** in Gaelic:

m' athair [maher] **my father/dad**

mo bhràthair [mo vraaher] **my brother**

When giving the name of a boy or man, you would say
'S e ... an t-ainm a th' air [sheh ... un tannam uh herr]
His name is... For example:

Seo mo bhràthair. 'S e Calum an t-ainm a th' air.
This is my brother. His name is Calum.

If you want to give their age, you say **Tha e ... bliadhna a dh'aois** [haa eh ... bleeyunuh uh goosh] **He is ... years old**.

The Gaelic word for **mother** or **mum** is **màthair** [maaher]. The word for **sister** is **piuthar** [pyoower]. Here is how you say **my mother/sister** in Gaelic:

mo mhàthair [mo vaaher] **my mother/mum**

mo phiuthar [mo fyoower] **my sister**

To tell someone the name of a girl or woman, say
'S e ... an t-ainm a th' oirre [sheh ... un tannam uh horruh]
Her name is... For example:

Seo mo phiuthar. 'S e Anna an t-ainm a th' oirre.
This is my sister. Her name is Anna.

To say how old they are, use the phrase **Tha i ... bliadhna a dh'aois** [haa ee ... bleeyunuh uh goosh] **She is ... years old**.

🔊 Listen to Track 2 / **Èist ri Traca 2**

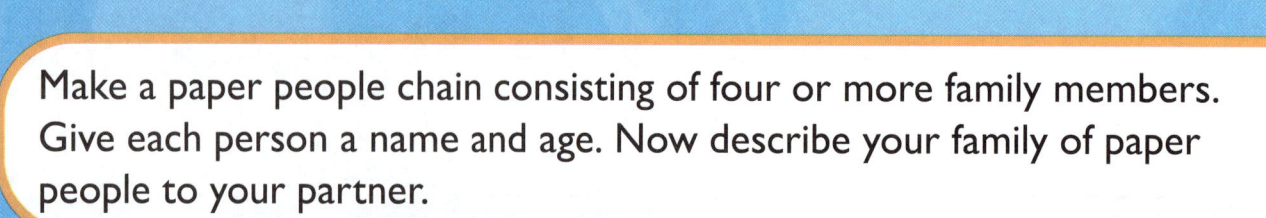

Make a paper people chain consisting of four or more family members. Give each person a name and age. Now describe your family of paper people to your partner.

Complete the profiles for your family below, giving the person's name and age, and drawing a **dealbh** (**picture**) of them. You might want to complete a profile for one of your friends instead: if so, you would use the phrase **Seo mo charaid** [shaw mo **ch**arritch] **This is my friend**.

Seo mo mhàthair.

'S e Màiri an t-ainm a th' oirre.

Tha i 34 bliadhna a dh'aois.

Seo _____

'S e _____

Tha _____

_____

_____

_____

_____

_____

_____

Cò ris a tha mi coltach?
What do I look like?

If you want to describe what you look like, you can use the phrase **Tha ... agam** [haa ... ackum], which means **I have...**, to talk about what colour eyes you have. The way to say this is by adding the colour adjective to the phrase below, for example: **Tha sùilean gorma agam. I have blue eyes.**

Tha sùilean ... agam.   [haa soolun ... ackum]   **I have ... eyes.**

gorma
[gorrumuh] **blue**

uaine
[ooanyuh] **green**

donna
[downuh] **brown**

To describe the colour and style of your hair, use the phrase **Tha ... orm** [haa ... orom] with some of the adjectives given below. For example: **Tha falt fada donn orm. I have long brown hair.**

Tha falt ... orm.   [haa falt ... orom]   **I have ... hair.**

donn
[down] **brown**

dubh
[doo] **black**

bàn
[baan] **blonde**

ruadh
[roo-ug] **red**

goirid
[gurritch] **short**

fada
[faduh] **long**

cùrlach
[curlo**ch**] **curly**

dìreach
[jeero**ch**] **straight**

🔊 Listen to Track 3 / **Èist ri Traca 3**

Play **Cò mi?** [koh mee] **Who am I?** with a partner. Think of someone you both know well and describe yourself as that person. You could give clues about the person's family or pets, for example: **Tha falt goirid bàn orm. Tha sùilean donna agam. Tha bràthair agam. Tha cù agam.** Your partner has to guess who you are describing.

Draw a picture of yourself in the box below. Answer the questions given below to write about your appearance in Gaelic. Remember to use **agam** when talking about your eye colour, and **orm** to talk about what your hair is like.

Mo dhealbh
My picture

Dè an t-ainm a th' ort?   Is mise_____
What's your name?

Cò ris a tha thu coltach?   Tha sùilean _____
What do you look like?

   Tha falt_____

Tha mi a' faireachdainn...
I feel...

When someone asks **Ciamar a tha thu?** [kimar uh haa oo] **How are you?**, it is useful to know a few phrases to say how you're feeling.

Tha mi toilichte.
[haa mee tawlee**ch**juh]
I'm happy.

Tha mi fiadhaich.
[haa mee feeyuh-ee**ch**]
I'm angry.

Tha mi brònach.
[haa mee brawno**ch**]
I'm sad.

Tha mi sgìth.
[haa mee skee]
I'm tired.

Tha an t-acras orm.
[haa un tackras orom]
I'm hungry.

Tha am pathadh orm.
[haa um paahi**g** orom]
I'm thirsty.

🔊 Listen to Track 4 / **Èist ri Traca 4**

Here are some more phrases to describe how you're feeling:
Tha mi gu math [haa mee goo mah] meaning **I'm well**
Tha mi tinn [haa mee cheen] meaning **I'm sick**
Tha an t-eagal orm [haa un checkul orom] meaning **I'm scared**
Tha mi air bhioran [haa mee err virrun] meaning **I'm excited**

Use paper plates to draw faces showing different emotions. Your partner asks **Ciamar a tha thu?** and you show one of your "faces" and say how you are feeling.

Write underneath each image how the person is feeling using **Tha mi...** or **Tha ... orm**.

An aimsir
The weather

We all like to talk about the weather and these phrases will help you to answer the question: **Ciamar a tha an aimsir an-diugh?** [kimar uh haa un amashir un joo] **What's the weather like today?**

Tha an t-uisge ann.
[haa un tooshguh aa-oon]
It's raining.

Tha i sgòthach.
[haa ee skaw-ho**ch**]
It's cloudy.

Tha i grianach.
[haa ee greeyuno**ch**]
It's sunny.

Tha i teth.
[haa ee chey]
It's hot.

Tha i fuar.
[haa ee foo-err]
It's cold.

Tha i gaothach.
[haa ee gooho**ch**]
It's windy.

🔊 Listen to Track 5 / **Èist ri Traca 5**

Look out of the window – how would you describe the weather today? **An-diugh tha...** [un joo haa] **Today it...** Now look up some other countries on the internet and describe the weather there.

Do you know...? **A bheil fios agad...?** The word **uisge** [ooshguh] in Gaelic can mean **rain**, but can also mean **water**.

Use the outline map of Scotland below to draw your own weather map using traditional weather symbols, then complete the sentences below the map with the appropriate weather phrases. Practise saying your weather report to a partner; you could even record or film yourself saying it!

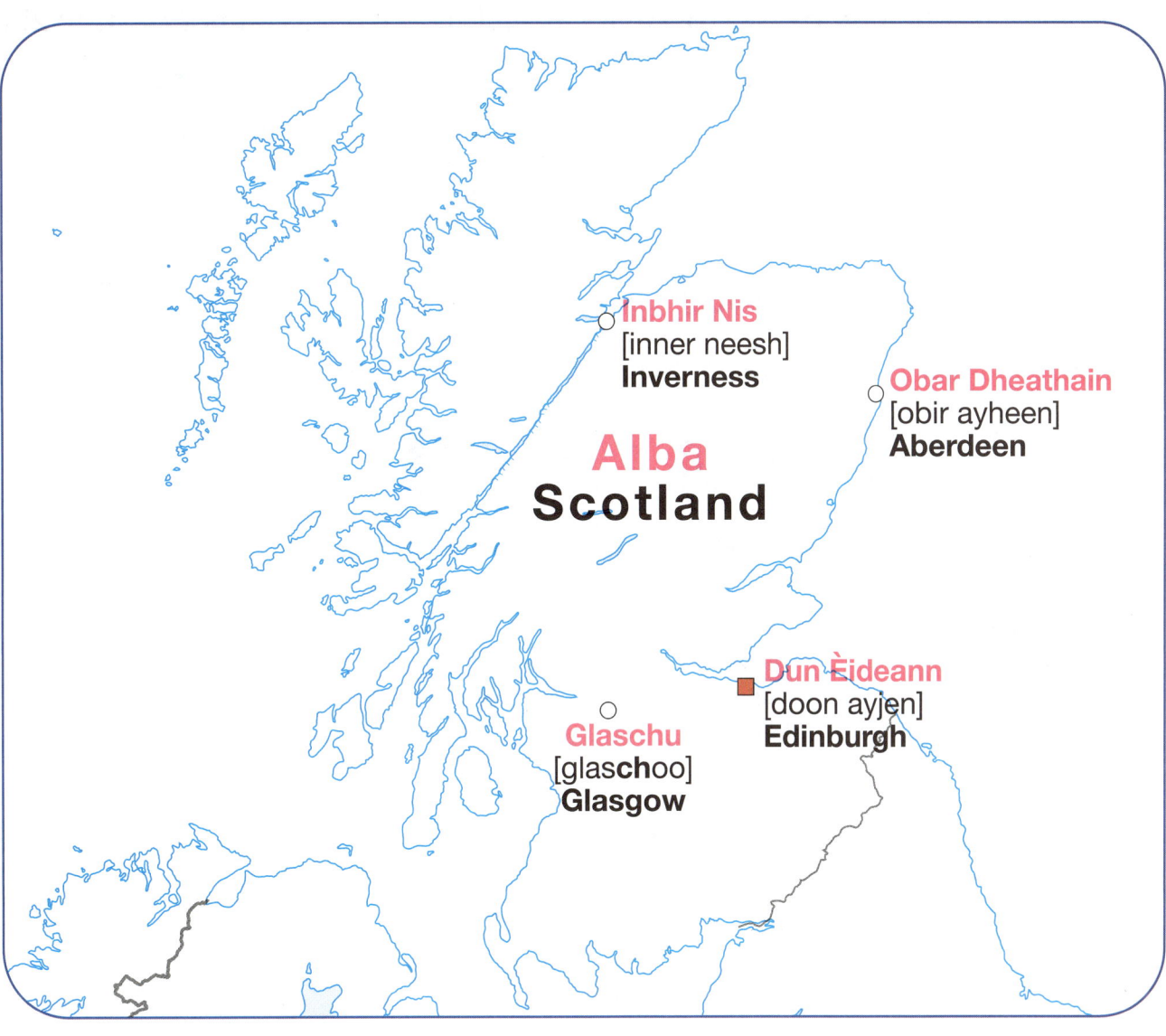

Inbhir Nis
[inner neesh]
Inverness

Obar Dheathain
[obir ayheen]
Aberdeen

Alba
Scotland

Dun Èideann
[doon ayjen]
Edinburgh

Glaschu
[glas**ch**oo]
Glasgow

Ann an... [aa-oon un] = In...

In Edinburgh...
Ann an Dun Èideann _____

In Glasgow...
Ann an Glaschu _____

In Inverness...
Ann an Inbhir Nis _____

In Aberdeen...
Ann an Obar Dheathain _____

Àireamhan gu 100
Numbers to 100

After learning the numbers 1 to 20, it's useful to learn the numbers after 20:

21 fichead 's a h-aon [fee**ch**it suh hunn]
22 fichead 's a dhà [fee**ch**it suh **g**aa]
23 fichead 's a trì [fee**ch**it suh tree]
24 fichead 's a ceithir [fee**ch**it suh kayher]
25 fichead 's a còig [fee**ch**it suh koeek]
26 fichead 's a sia [fee**ch**it suh shia]
27 fichead 's a seachd [fee**ch**it suh sha**ch**k]
28 fichead 's a h-ochd [fee**ch**it suh ho**ch**k]
29 fichead 's a naoi [fee**ch**it suh nuee]
30 trithead [tree**ch**it]
31 trithead 's a h-aon [tree**ch**it suh hunn]
40 ceathrad [kerrit]
50 caogad [koogit]
60 seasgad [shessgit]
70 seachdad [sha**ch**kit]
80 ochdad [o**ch**kit]
90 naochad [noo**ch**it]
100 ceud [keeyud]

🔊 Listen to Track 6 / **Èist ri Traca 6**

For all numbers between the tens, like **21** to **29**, you add **'s a** or **'s a h-** between the larger number and the smaller one. For example, **41** would be **ceathrad 's a h-aon** [kerrit suh hunn], **42** would be **ceathrad 's a dhà** [kerrit suh **g**aa] and so on.

Practise counting in tens, backwards and forwards, loudly and quietly, slowly and quickly. You could also try counting up in twos, threes or fives, either by yourself or with a partner.

Work out the sums and write the answers in Gaelic. Then colour in **an ròbot** [an robot] using the colour key provided.

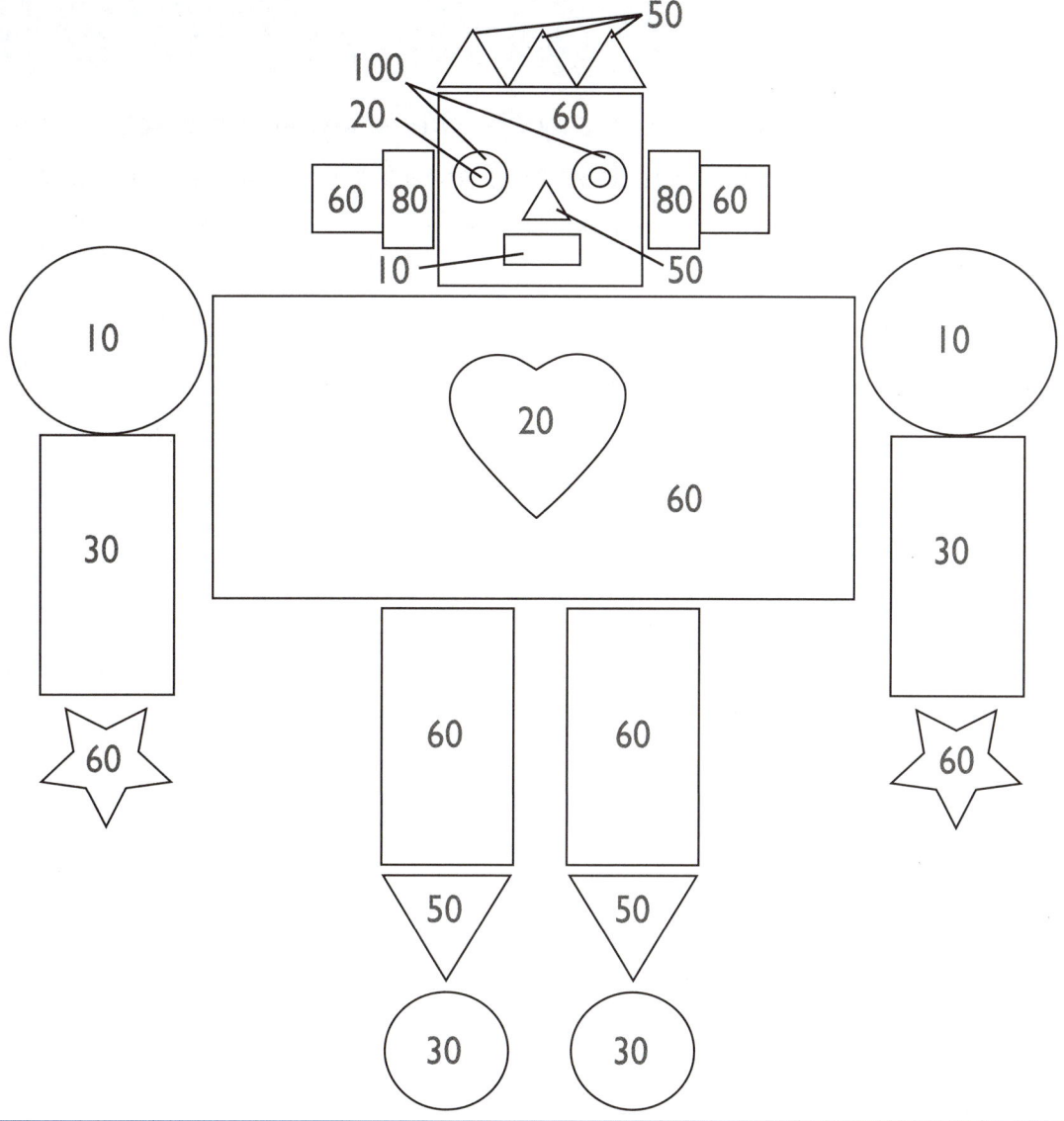

Suimeannan Sums	Freagairtean Answers	Dath Colour
deich cuir-ris **fichead**	trithead	**uaine**
seasgad thoir-air-falbh **ceathrad**		**dearg**
trithead thoir-air-falbh **fichead**		**orains**
ceathrad cuir-ris **ceathrad**		**purpaidh**
seachdad cuir-ris **trithead**		**dubh**
ceud thoir-air-falbh **caogad**		**buidhe**
ochdad thoir-air-falbh **fichead**		**gorm**

(cuir-ris = add; thoir-air-falbh = take away)

Làithean na seachdaine/Mìosan
Days of the week/Months

It is useful to know how to say the days of the week and months of the year in Gaelic. Like English, you write days and months with a capital letter.

Diluain	[jeelooeen]	Monday
Dimàirt	[jeemaarsht]	Tuesday
Diciadain	[jeekeeyudeen]	Wednesday
Diardaoin	[jurshduh-een]	Thursday
Dihaoine	[jeehuh-nyuh]	Friday
Disathairne	[jeesaharnyuh]	Saturday
Didòmhnaich	[jeedawnee**ch**]	Sunday

Am Faoilleach	[um fuhllyo**ch**]	January
An Gearran	[un gyarran]	February
Am Màrt	[um maarsht]	March
An Giblean	[un geebleen]	April
An Cèitean	[un kaychan]	May
An t-Ògmhios	[un tog vee-us]	June
An t-Iuchar	[un choo**ch**ar]	July
An Lùnastal	[un loonasdal]	August
An t-Sultain	[un toolteen]	September
An Dàmhair	[un daavir]	October
An t-Samhain	[un taween]	November
An Dùbhlachd	[un doolo**ch**k]	December

Here are some more words you may find useful:

latha	[laa-uh]	day
mìos	[mee-us]	month
an-diugh	[un joo]	today

🔊 Listen to Track 7 / **Èist ri Traca 7**

The Gaelic word for **date** is **ceann-latha** [kya-oon laa-uh], and your **birthday** is your **co-là-breith** [koh laa bray]. A simple way to write the date in Gaelic is just to give the number, and then the month without the **An/Am/An t-** in front, for example:

8th April = **8 Giblean**

Write out the names of days of the week or months on separate pieces of paper. Mix them up and then try to put them back into the correct order as quickly as possible. Why not challenge your partner to beat your time?

Geama: Faclan-falaichte

Can you find some of the Gaelic days of the week and months in the square?

Diluain **Màrt**

Dàmhair **Dihaoine**

Cèitean **Ògmhios**

Diciadain **Gearran**

Diardaoin **Lùnastal**

D	Ò	D	I	L	U	A	I	N	L	I
N	F	À	I	Ù	H	M	À	R	T	A
S	R	M	Ì	H	S	P	A	N	B	A
O	R	H	A	B	A	L	I	M	C	L
I	Ò	A	R	M	C	O	H	C	È	A
H	A	I	G	R	A	M	I	R	I	T
M	Ì	R	C	D	A	E	À	N	T	S
G	F	H	R	C	Ù	A	D	M	E	A
Ò	N	A	R	G	E	A	R	R	A	N
U	I	A	M	N	H	G	D	L	N	Ù
D	I	C	I	A	D	A	I	N	P	L

Why not make up your own puzzle using some of the Gaelic words for months or days of the week?

_____

_____

_____

_____

Cur-seachadan
Pastimes

When talking to someone in Gaelic you might want to say what kinds of things you enjoy or don't enjoy.

Is toil leam... [iss tullum...] **I like...**
Cha toil leam... [**ch**a tullum] **I don't like...**

snàmh
[snaav]
swimming

rothaireachd
[roharro**ch**k]
cycling

ball-coise
[bahl koshuh]
football

leughadh
[layvi**g**]
reading

peantadh
[penti**g**]
painting

geamaichean bhidio
[gemmee**ch**in video]
video games

🔊 Listen to Track 8 / **Èist ri Traca 8**

If you feel even more strongly, you can say **'S fhìor thoil leam...** [sheer hullum] **I really like...** and **'S lugha orm...** [slu**g**uh orom] **I hate...**

Work with a partner: one person says what they like or don't like doing using **Is toil leam...** [iss tullum] or **Cha toil leam...** [**ch**a tullum]. The other person has to mime the activity described, but only if their partner likes doing it. If they don't like doing it, you don't mime it, so listen carefully!

Do you know...? **A bheil fios agad...?** A popular game in many parts of Scotland is **shinty**, or **camanachd** [kamano**ch**k] in Gaelic. It is a bit like hockey: players must try and hit a ball with a stick called a **caman** (the same word is used in English and Gaelic). Unlike hockey, you can hit the ball in the air.

Use the outline below to design a **sgiath** [skia] – your own personal shield with your coat of arms. In each section draw one of your hobbies and then write below what it is in Gaelic, using **Is toil leam...** or **'S fhìor thoil leam...** Why not try and find out some more words for different hobbies in Gaelic by using a dictionary or by searching online?

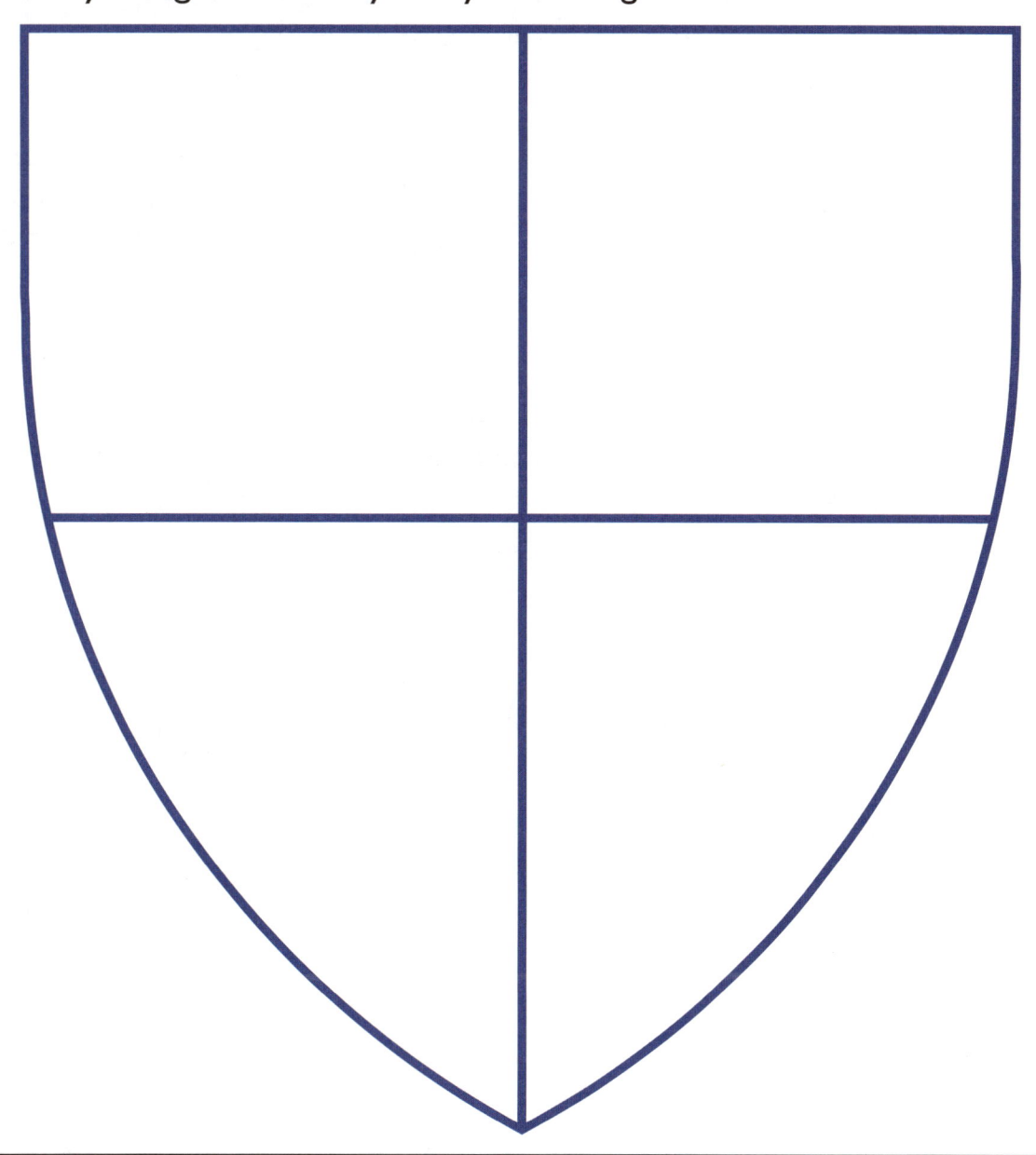

Is toil leam... / 'S fhìor thoil leam...

-
-
-
-

Biadh
Food

It's always fun to talk about the food you like in a new language. Here are some words for foods you may have throughout the day:

Bracaist [brackashtch] Breakfast

aran [arran] bread

silidh [sheelee] jam

gràinean bracaist [graanyen brackashtch] breakfast cereal

Lòn [lawn] Lunch

ceapaire [keparuh] sandwich

brot [brot] soup

sliseagan [shleeshackin] chips

Dìnnear [jeenar] Dinner

cearc [kyark] chicken

iasg [eeusk] fish

piotsa [peetsa] pizza

buntàta [boontaatuh] potato(es)

curranan [kooranin] carrots

sailead [salad] salad

Greimeagan [graymackin] Snacks

ubhal [oo-ul] apple

orainsear [orenshar] orange

cèic [kehk] cake

🔊 Listen to Track 9 / **Èist ri Traca 9**

The phrase **Bu toil leam...** [boo tullum] in Gaelic means **I would like...**, for example: **Bu toil leam piotsa** [boo tullum peetsa] **I would like pizza.** If you want to ask someone what they would like, you say **Dè bu toil leat?** [jay boo tullat] **What would you like?**

Fill in the gaps to complete the shopping list in Gaelic.

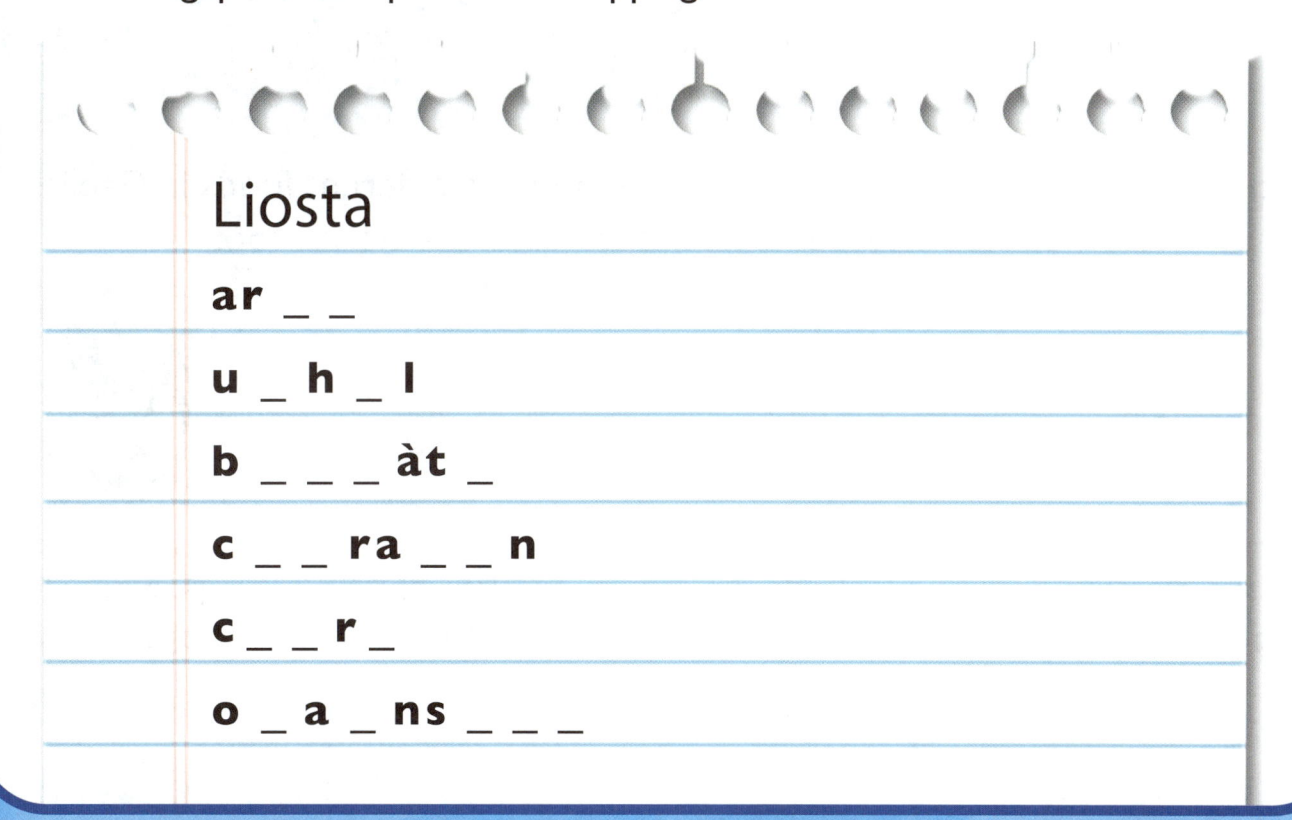

Liosta

ar _ _

u _ h _ l

b _ _ _ àt _

c _ _ ra _ _ n

c _ _ r _

o _ a _ ns _ _ _

Read what each child wants for dinner and draw it onto the plates in front of them. One of the children has only thought of two things – add another food item and draw it on the plate.

Cearc, buntàta agus curranan.

Ceapaire, sliseagan agus cèic.

Piotsa, sailead agus _____ .

Deoch
Drink

Now that you have learned some of the words for different foods in Gaelic, you will also want to know some names for different drinks, too:

sùgh orainsear
[soo orenshar]
orange juice

cofaidh
[coffee]
coffee

teatha
[tayuh]
tea

sùgh ubhal
[soo oo-ul]
apple juice

teòclaid teth
[chocklatch chey]
hot chocolate

deoch-liomaide
[jo**ch** leematchuh]
lemonade

bainne
[banyuh]
milk

uisge
[ooshguh]
water

🔊 Listen to Track 10 / **Èist ri Traca 10**

To say what you want to drink in Gaelic, you can use the phrase **Tha mi ag iarraidh...** [haa mee uh geeyuree] **I want...** When someone offers you something to drink (or eat), they might say **A bheil thu ag iarraidh...?** [uh vel oo uh geeyuree] **Do you want...?** You would answer by saying **tha** [haa] for **yes** and **chan eil** [**ch**an yel] for **no**.

With a partner, use the phrases you have learned to pretend you are ordering food and drinks in a café. Remember to use **mas e do thoil e** [mass eh daw holl eh] for **please** and **tapadh leat** [tapuh lat] to say **thank you**.

Design a **menu** or **clàr-bìdh** [klaar beeyee] for a hotel, written in Gaelic. Include **deochan** (**drinks**), **bracaist** (**breakfast**), **lòn** (**lunch**) and **dìnnear** (**dinner**) – perhaps some **mìlsean** (**desserts**) too! If you want to include your own vocabulary, use a dictionary to help you.

Clàr-bìdh

Na rudan as fheàrr leam
My favourite things

When you are talking about your favourite things in Gaelic – for example colours, animals, food, or hobbies – you can use the phrases below.

'S e ... an dath as fheàrr leam.
[sheh ... un dah uh sharr lum]
My favourite colour is...

'S e ... am biadh as fheàrr leam.
[sheh ... um beeyug uh sharr lum]
My favourite food is...

'S e ... an cur-seachad as fheàrr leam.
[sheh ... un koor-shachid uh sharr lum]
My favourite hobby is...

'S e ... am peata as fheàrr leam.
[sheh ... um pettuh uh sharr lum]
My favourite pet is...

Make a paper "fortune teller" (**cairt an fhortain**) using numbers on the outside, colours on the inner layer and either a picture or word for a food, animal or hobby on the inside. Use it to play with a partner – when you open up the inside, it will show which one is your favourite.

Geama: Geama a' chrochaire

Play "Hangman" (**Geama a' chrochaire**) using the words you have been learning. First of all agree on the category, for example, **biadh**, **dathan**, **làithean** or **teaghlach**, then choose a Gaelic word from this category.

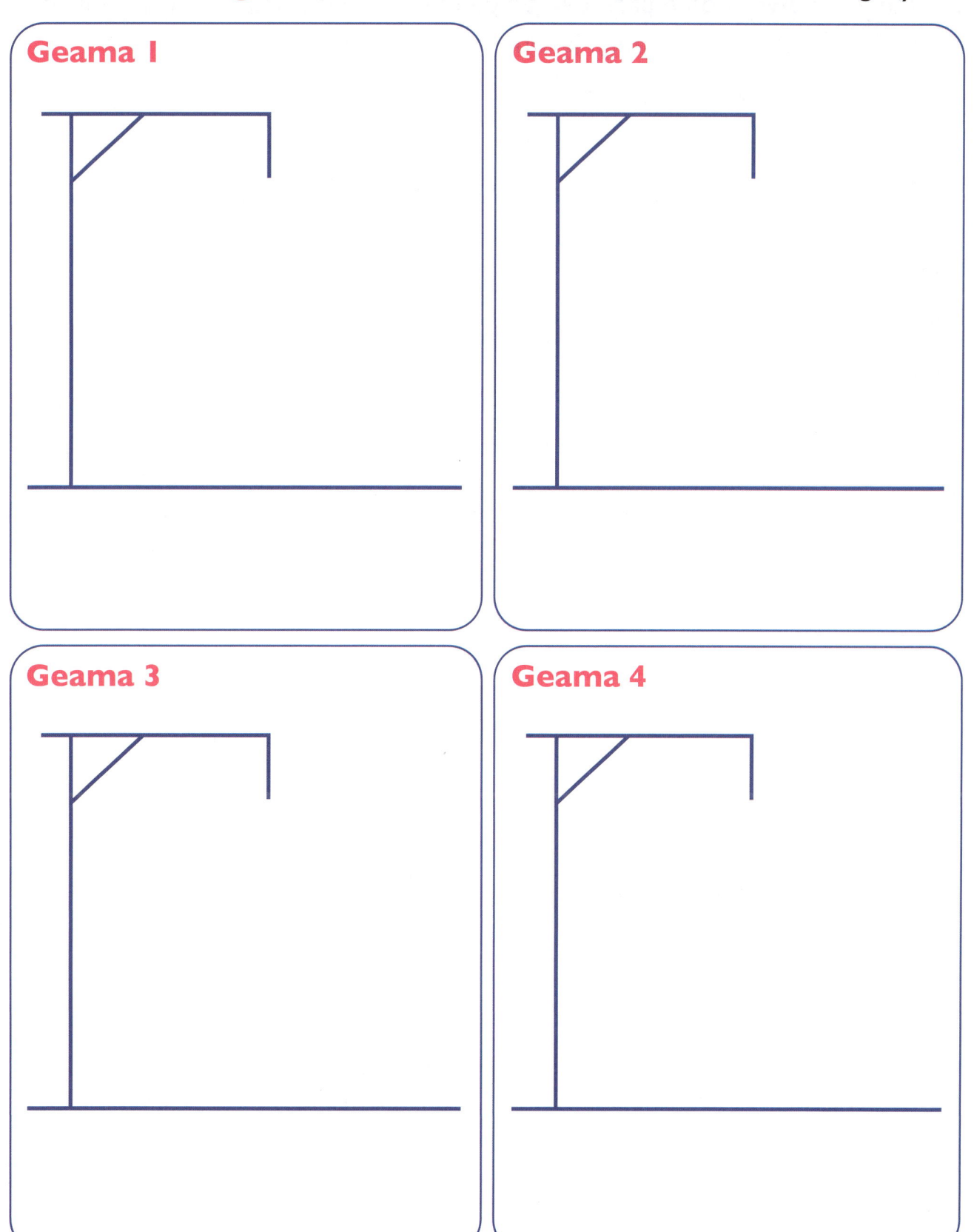

Geama 1

Geama 2

Geama 3

Geama 4

Mi fhìn
About me

Create your own profile page by completing the template below, adding in information about family, pets, favourite foods, and hobbies.

Ainm: _____

Aois: _____

Co-là-breith: _____

Tha sùilean _____

Tha falt _____
_____

Dealbh

Mo theaghlach
Tha ... agam.

Peataichean
Tha ... agam.

Biadh agus deoch
Is toil leam...
-
-
-

Cha toil leam...
-
-
-

Cur-seachadan
Is toil leam...
-
-
-

Cha toil leam...
-
-
-

Geama: Geama-bùird

Here is a game you could play with one or more other players. You will need a **dìsinn** (**a die**) and **cunntairean** [koontarin] (**counters**). **Roilig sia** (**roll a six**) to get started. **Gur math a thèid leat!** Good luck!

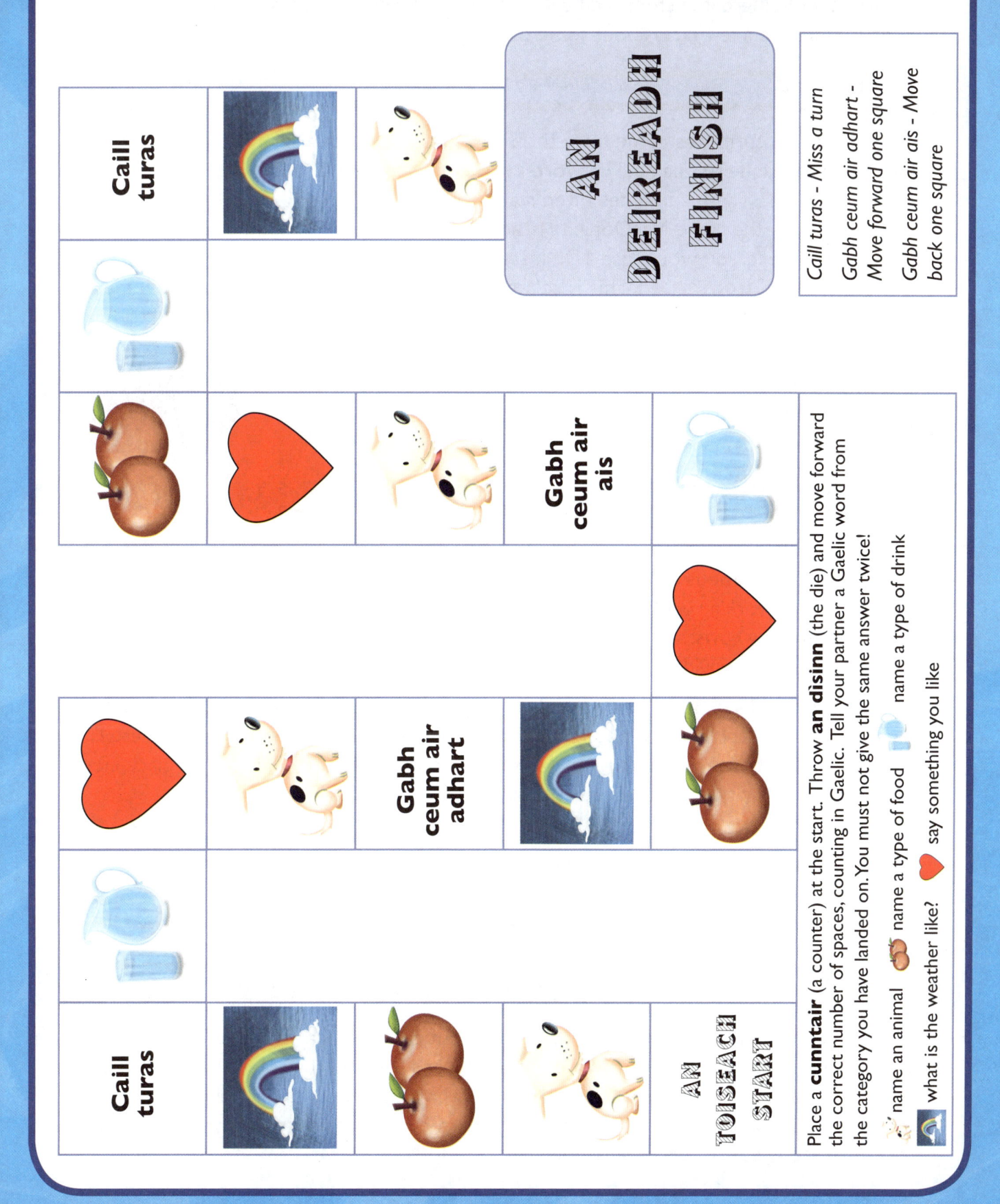

Caill turas - Miss a turn
Gabh ceum air adhart - Move forward one square
Gabh ceum air ais - Move back one square

AN DEIREADH / FINISH

Board squares (from START, following path):
- AN TOISEACH / START
- dog
- apples
- rainbow
- Caill turas
- jug & glass
- heart
- dog
- Gabh ceum air adhart
- rainbow
- apples
- heart
- heart
- jug & glass
- apples
- Gabh ceum air ais
- dog
- heart
- apples
- jug & glass
- rainbow
- dog
- Caill turas

Place a **cunntair** (a counter) at the start. Throw **an dìsinn** (the die) and move forward the correct number of spaces, counting in Gaelic. Tell your partner a Gaelic word from the category you have landed on. You must not give the same answer twice!

- 🐶 name an animal
- 🍎 name a type of food
- 🧃 name a type of drink
- ❤️ say something you like
- 🌈 what is the weather like?

Traidiseanan agus cultar
Traditions and culture

There are lots of different customs and events that are important to Gaels and Scots all over the world. Here are a few facts about some of these traditions and celebrations.

- Lots of Scottish surnames come from the Scottish clans, which are large family groups who share the same last name. The word **clan** comes from a Gaelic word, **clann**, which means "children". These surnames often start with Mac or Mc – the word **mac** in Gaelic means "son", so the name MacDonald (**MacDhòmhnaill** in Gaelic) means "son of Donald". In Gaelic, you would use **Nic** instead of **Mac** in your surname if you are a girl or woman: **NicDhòmhnaill**. This is related to the Gaelic word **nighean**, which means "daughter".

- Lots of clans have a clan tartan. Tartan cloth is often used to make kilts (known as the **fèileadh** in Gaelic) – many people who wear kilts choose to wear one made in their clan tartan. The Gaelic word for **tartan** is **breacan**.

- Music, especially singing, is an important part of Gaelic culture and different types of songs were sung during various activities. For example, **òrain-luaidh** (waulking songs) were sung by people working with tweed or cloth, **òrain-bhleoghain** (milking songs) were sung when milking cows, and **puirt-à-beul** (mouth music) is a fast, rhythmic type of singing that people would dance to.

- A **mòd** (or **mod** in English) is a type of gathering where Gaelic speakers of all ages come together to take part in music, poetry and literature competitions. The biggest of these is **the Royal National Mod** (**am Mòd Nàiseanta Rìoghail**), which takes place in a different town or city in Scotland every October.

- A **ceilidh** (or **cèilidh**) is an evening of music, singing and Scottish country dancing. Traditional Gaelic cèilidhs are often organised by a host, known as **fear/bean an taighe** (the **man/woman of the house**), who will introduce performers and tell stories or jokes.

- Christmas is widely celebrated in Scotland today, but the New Year is just as special for many people. Hogmanay is an old Scots word for New Year's Eve, and the Gaelic name for this is **Oidhche Challainn**. It was traditional for children to get dressed up and visit neighbours to ask for treats and sweets, which they would earn by singing a song or saying a rhyme, like trick-or-treating at Halloween time now!

Cumaibh oirbh!
Keep going!

This page gives some suggestions for games and activities that can be used for continued language practice, either with individual children, or a larger group.

It is often useful to have some basic commands in Gaelic and some of these listed below may be helpful. All the instructions are listed first in the singular and then in the plural, depending on whether you are addressing one child or several. There are also a few phrases you can use to encourage children as they play and learn.

Seall! [shaa-ool]	**Seallaibh!** [shalliv]	**Look!**
Èist! [ayshj]	**Èistibh!** [ayshjiv]	**Listen!**
Seas! [shess]	**Seasaibh!** [shessiv]	**Stand up!**
Suidh! [sooy]	**Suidhibh!** [sooyiv]	**Sit down!**
Tòisich! [tawshee**ch**]	**Tòisichibh!** [tawshee**ch**iv]	**Start!**
Stad! [stat]	**Stadaibh!** [stativ]	**Stop!**
Siuthad! [shoo-ud]	**Siuthadaibh!** [shoo-ujiv]	**Go on!**

It is always good to encourage children positively as they learn. Here are some Gaelic phrases you could use to do so:

| **'S math a rinn thu!** [smah uh ruyn oo] | **'S math a rinn sibh!** [smah uh ruyn shiv] | **Well done!** |
| **Cùm ort!** [coom orsht] | **Cumaibh oirbh!** [coomiv urriv] | **Keep going!** |

Glè mhath! [glay vah] **Very good!**
'S math sin! [smah shin] **That's great!**
Sgoinneil! [sgunyal] **Fantastic!**

Active games, played indoors or outdoors, are a great way of reinforcing learning as well as having fun in Gaelic:

- Two rows of children must sit facing each other, stretching their legs out so that their feet touch to form a human "ladder". Make sure there is space between the pairs. Each pair is given a Gaelic word (number, colour, animal, etc) and when their word is called out they have to run over the legs, round the outside and back to their place as quickly as possible. Teammates can encourage their runner in Gaelic by shouting **Siuthad!**

- Children form teams of 4 or 5 and stand at one end of the area. At the other end there are several large pieces of paper, one for each team. On each of these pieces of paper are written Gaelic numbers, colours, letters or whatever is being practised. When one of these Gaelic words is called, the first team member has to run to the paper and circle the correct one. To make it more fun, if the word that has been called out isn't on the paper, the child has to do five star jumps!

- "Chinese whispers" – pass a sentence in Gaelic round the circle and see what it sounds like at the end. How close does it sound to the original? Where did it all go wrong?

'S math a rinn thu! You have learned how to say so many things in Gaelic. Colour in the letters and pictures and fill in your name and date to make your very own personalised certificate.

Teisteanas Gàidhlig

Math dha-rìribh!

Tha Gàidhlig aig

Ainm / Name: _____

Ceann-latha / Date: _____